Failures of Risk management

Preface

I0467588

A large loss is not evidence of a risk management failure because a large loss can happen even if risk management is flawless. Risk management failures show how various types of risk management failures occur. Because of the limitations of past data in assessing the probability and the implications of a financial crisis, we conclude that financial institutions

drpriyarawal@gmail.com

should use scenarios for credible financial crisis threats even if they perceive the probability of such events to be extremely small. The significance of according priority and resources towards Disaster Risk Reduction ("DRR") for India arises from the fact that India is amongst the most disaster prone counties in the world. India is subject to various types of disasters including earthquakes, cyclones, tsunami, floods, landslides etc. The fact that it is a developing country also implies greater vulnerability and lower resilience to disasters. According to the World Bank India loses up to 2% of its GDP and 12%government revenue to direct losses arising from disasters.

Dr.Priya Rawal

drpriyarawal@gmail.com

Acknowledgements

Without the unconditional love of my brother **Mr. Puneet Kumar Rawal**, my parents **Mr. K.V.S Rawal (father)**&**S.K Rawal (mother)**, I would not have dared to begin and complete my book. They have always been on my side and backed me to fulfill my desires in anything I choose to pursue. I have got to be grateful to my beloved family members, friends and well-wishers for the constant inspiration, support and

drpriyarawal@gmail.com

4

prayers they rendered for the completion of this work. Last but not the least; I kneel down in profound humility and deep gratitude before **The Lord Almighty** for showering **His** blessings and grace on me through all the stages of this humble endeavor and thereafter.

Dr.Priya Rawal

drpriyarawal@gmail.com

Index

Chapter-1

Introduction

In commentaries on the financial crisis that started during the summer of 2007, a constant refrain is that somehow risk management failed and that there were risk management failures at financial institutions across the world. For instance, an article in the Financial Times states that "it is obvious that there has been a massive failure of risk management across most of Wall Street."' In this article, we want to examine what it means for risk management to fail. We show that the fact that an institution makes an extremely large loss does not imply that risk management failed or that the institution made a mistake. This article does not examine the subprime financial crisis or problems of financial institutions during that crisis directly. Rather, it is an attempt to make sure that if risk management is blamed, it is for the right reasons. Otherwise, changes in risk management that take place in response to the crisis might be counterproductive and top executives and investors could keep expecting more from risk management than what it can actually deliver. To examine risk management failures more concretely, we go back to the problems experienced by the hedge fund LTCM in 1998 to analyse how one might conclude that the failure of LTCM was a risk management failure or not. We then generalize from that example to describe what constitutes a risk management failure and what does not. We will show that some events considered in the financial press to be risk management failures actually are not risk management failures, but at the same time we will analyse many different ways in which risk management can fail. We then address the question of whether lessons from risk management failures can be used to help improve the practice of risk management. In the last part of this article, we discuss an approach to risk management that might enable institutions to better manage risks such as those that threatened them during the subprime financial crisis.

Chapter-2

Was the collapse of Long-Term Capital Management a risk management failure?

The story of Long-Term Capital Management (LTCM) is well-known. In 1994, ex-Salomon Brothers traders and two future Nobel Prize winners started a hedge fund, the Long-Term Capital Fund. LTCM was the company that managed the fund. The fund performed superbly for most of its life: Investors earned 20% for ten months in 1994, 43% in 1995, 41% in 1996, and 17% in1997. In August and September 1998, following the default of Russia on its rubble denominated debt, world capital markets were in crisis and the hedge fund LTCM lost most of its capital. Before its collapse, LTCM had capital close to $5 billion, assets in excess of $100 billion, and derivatives for a notional amount in excess of $1 trillion. By mid-September, LTCM's capital had fallen by more than $3.5 billion and the Federal Reserve Bank of New York coordinated a rescue by private financial institutions that injected $3.65 billion in the fund. Does a loss of more than 70% of capital represent a risk management failure? Does a loss that requires a rescue by banks involving an injection of $3.65 billion of new capital show that risk management failed? It turns out that it is not easy to answer these questions. To define a risk management failure, one must first define the role of risk management. In a typical firm, the role of risk management is first to assess the risks faced by the firm, communicate these risks to those who make risk-taking decisions for the firm, and finally manage and monitor those risks to make sure that the firm only bears the risks its management and board of directors want it to bear. In general, a firm will specify a risk measure that it focuses on together with additional risk metrics. When that risk measure exceeds the firm's tolerance for risk, risk is reduced. Alternatively, when the risk measure is too low for the firm's risk tolerance, the firm increases its risk. Because firms are generally more concerned about unexpected losses, a frequently used risk measure is Value-at-Risk or VaR, a measure of downside risk. VaR is the maximum loss at a given confidence level over a given period of time. Hence, if the 95% confidence level is used and a firm has a one-day VaR of $150 million, the firm has a 5% chance of making a loss in excess of $150 million over the next day if the VaR is correctly estimated. This measure might be estimated daily or over longer periods of time. Even with our definition of the role of risk management, the returns of LTCM do not tell us anything about whether its risk management failed. To understand why, it is helpful to consider a very simple hypothetical example. Suppose that you stood in the shoes of the managers of LTC Min January 1998 and had the opportunity to invest in trades that, overall, had a 99% chance of producing a return for the fund before fees of 25% and a 1% chance of making a loss of 70% over the coming year. Though this example is hypothetical, it is plausible in light of the returns of LTCM and what LTCM was telling its investors. First, in its two best years the fund earned more than 50% before fees, so that a return of 25% does not sound implausible. Second, LTCM wrote to its investors to tell them that it expected that the fund would experience a loss in excess of 20% only in one year out of 50 - here; instead, one year out of 100 can be expected to have a loss of 10%? Let's assume that whether the fund had the high return or not depended on the flip of a weighted coin, so that the risk of the fund would have been completely diversifiable for its investors. With this hypothetical example, the expected return on the fund would then have been24.05%. Such an expected return would have been a great expected return for a hedge fund or for any investment as this would have been the expected return for bearing diversifiable risk, given my assumptions. Had the managers had the opportunity to keep repeating this investment, 99 years out of 100 they would have earned 25% before fees and would have been stars? In my hypothetical example, when the managers of the funds (the partners) made their choice, they knew the true distribution of possible outcomes of the fund. Hence, they knew the distribution of gains and losses perfectly - the risk managers should have earned a gold medal for their work. Suppose, however, that the bad outcome occurs. In this case, the fund would have made headlines for having lost $3.5 billion. Some would argue that the risk of the fund was poorly managed. However, by construction, risk management could not have been improved in this case. The managers knew exactly the risks they faced - and they decided to take them. Therefore, there is no sense in which risk management failed. Ex post, the only argument one could make is that the managers took risks they should not have, but that is not a risk management issue as long as the risks

21

were properly understood. Rather, it is an issue of assessing the costs of losses versus the gains from making large profits. Deciding whether to take a known risk is not a decision for risk managers. The decision depends on the risk appetite of an institution. However, defining the risk appetite is a decision for the board and top management. That decision is at the heart of the firm's strategy and of how it creates value for its shareholders. A decision to take a known risk may turn out poorly even though, at the time it was made, the expectation was that taking the risk increased shareholder wealth and hence was in the best interest of the shareholders. In the case of LTCM, it could be argued that the cost of losing $3.5 billion for the investor's in LTCM was just that - namely, there were no additional costs beyond the direct monetary loss. For most firms, however, large losses have deadweight costs. These deadweight costs are at the foundation of financial theories of why risk management creates shareholder wealth. "If a financial institution makes a large loss, the institution may, for instance, have to scale back its investments because of being financially constrained, have to sell assets in unfavourable markets, lose valuable employees who become concerned for their bonuses, lose customers who are concerned about the institution being distracted or not having sufficient resources to help them, and face increased scrutiny from regulators. In any institution, the board and top management have to take into account these deadweight costs of large losses when making decisions that create the risk of large losses. Risk managers can estimate whether an action is profitable for the firm given its risk appetite because they can evaluate how much capital is required to support that action.' However, an action that is not profitable for a given level of risk appetite can become profitable if the firm's risk appetite increases because less capital is required to support that action. Whether taking large risks is worthwhile for an institution ultimately depends on the firm's strategy. Risk managers do not set strategy. Suppose that a firm sets its risk appetite by choosing a target credit rating. Such an approach is well-established. Once the credit rating is chosen, there are multiple combinations of risk and capital that achieve the target rating. For a given choice of leverage, the firm does not have much choice in choosing its risk level if it wants to achieve its target rating. However, faced with good opportunities, the firm could choose to have less leverage so that it can bear more risk or it could choose to depart from its credit rating target. LTCM provides a good example of such trade-offs. In the fall of 1997, the managers of LTCM concluded that they did not want to manage a business earning 17% for its investors, which is what their investors had earned for the year. Instead, they wanted the higher returns achieved in 1995 and 1996. At the end of 1997, LTCM had capital of $7.4 billion but decided to return roughly 36% of the capital to its investors. With less capital, LTCM could still execute the same trades. However, now, to implement them it had to borrow more and hence had to increase its leverage. By increasing its leverage, it could boost the return to its shareholders if things went well at the expense of making more losses if things went poorly. Was increasing leverage a poor risk management decision? In my example, the partners of LTCM knew the risks and the rewards from doing so. In the well-worn language of financial economics, increasing leverage was a positive NPV decision when it was made, but obviously ex post it was a costly decision as it meant that when assets fell in value, the fund's equity fell in value faster than it would have with less leverage. There has been much discussion of incentives of top management during the credit crisis, with various commentators arguing that part of the problem has been that top management had incentives to take too much risk. This may well be so, but before reaching conclusions one should not forget that financial economists have argued for decades that incentives of management become better aligned with those of shareholders when management has a large stake in the firm's equity. Top management owned hundreds of millions of dollars of equity in Bear Stearns and Lehman at the peak of the valuation of these firms. Similarly, the partners of LTCM collectively had almost $2 billion invested in the fund at the beginning of 1998. If such equity stakes do not incentivize managers to make the right decisions for their shareholders, what would? In summary, risk management does not prevent losses. With good risk management, large losses can occur when those making the risk-taking decisions conclude that taking large, well-understood risks creates value for their organization.

Chapter-3

Risk measures and risk management failures

A widely used risk measure in financial institutions is a daily VaR measure for trading activities. Large banks usually disclose data on that measure quarterly. They will generally say the number of times in a quarter the P&L had a loss that exceeds the daily VaR. For instance, UBS reported in its annual report for 2006 that it never had a loss that exceeded its daily VaR. In contrast, in 2007, it reported in its annual report that it exceeded its daily VaR 29 times. The results for 2007 show that fundamental changes were taking place in the economy that made it difficult for risk managers to track risk on a daily basis. However, such a large number of VaR exceedances provide little or no information about the implication of these exceedances for the financial health of UBS. It could be that the exceedances were really small and that there were many large gains as well because volatility increased rapidly. Alternatively, there could have been very large losses and few large gains. In the former case, the firm could be ahead at the end of the year. In the latter case, it could be in serious trouble. Consequently, focusing on the daily market VaR, though intellectually satisfying for risk managers because the most up-to-date quantitative techniques can be brought to bear on the problem, can only be one part of risk management and not the one that top management should focus on. Top management has to focus on the longer-run implications of risk. Short-run VaR measures can be low and the firm can appear to do an extremely good job with them, yet it can fail. I have not seen monthly VaR estimates from LTCM. However, from March 1994 to December 1997, LTCM had only eight months with losses and the worst monthly loss was 2.9%. In contrast, it had 37 months with gains.'"

As a result, one would have a hard time using historical monthly returns to conclude that its risk management was flawed. Consider a firm that has a one-day VaR of $100 million for its trading book at the 1% probability level. This means that the firm has a one percent chance of losing more than $100 million. If this firm exceeded its VaR once over 100 trading days and lost $10 billion, all existing statistical tests of risk management performance based on VaR exceedances would indicate that the firm has excellent risk management. VaR does not capture catastrophic losses that have a small probability of occurring. Daily VaR measures assume that assets can be sold quickly or hedged, so that a firm can limit its losses essentially within a day. However, both in 1998 and over the last year, we have seen that markets can become suddenly less liquid, so that daily VaR measures lose their meaning. If a firm sits on a portfolio that cannot be traded, a daily VaR measure is not a measure of the risk of the portfolio because the firm is stuck with the portfolio for a much longer period of time. To assess risk, firms have to look at longer horizons and have to take a comprehensive view of their risks.

A one-year horizon is widely used in enterprise risk management for measures of firm-wide risk. Generally, financial institutions that focus on firm-wide risk at a one-year horizon aim for credit ratings that imply an extremely small probability of default.

Such approaches are useful in assessing a firm's risk, in estimating the optimal amount of capital for a firm, and estimating the profitability of projects and lines of business through a careful evaluation of the cost of the capital required to bear their risks. However, at the same time, such approaches are not sufficient. A high target credit rating effectively means that the firm tries to avoid default in all but the most extreme circumstances. If a firm aims for an AA credit rating, it effectively chooses a probability of default which is such that it would default less frequently than one year out of a allows it to survive crises. Further, the probability of a crisis is difficult to estimate precisely, so that even if the estimate of the probability is very small, estimation error could be such that the true, unknown, probability is much higher. Consequently, the firm has to focus on crisis events in its risk measurement and management. Existing risk models are generally not designed to capture risks associated with crises and to help firms manage them. These models use historical data and are most precise for short horizons - like days. With short horizons, crises are extremely rare events. Yet, when we consider years, crises are not extremely rare events. Months and years are a better horizon to evaluate risk when it comes to crises for at least two reasons. First, as evidenced since the summer of 2007, crises involve a dramatic withdrawal of liquidity from the markets. The withdrawal of liquidity means that firms are stuck with positions that they never expected to hold for a long time because price pressure costs involved in trading out of these positions are extremely high. Positions whose risk was evaluated over one day because the firm thought it could trade out of these positions suddenly became positions that had to be held for weeks or months. Second, during crisis periods, firms will make multiple losses that exceed their daily

VaR and these losses can be large enough to substantially weaken them. As a result, risk measures have to contemplate the distribution of large losses over time rather than over one day. Crises involve complicated interactions across risks and across institutions. Statistical risk models typically take returns to be exogenous to the firm and ignore risk concentrations across institutions. Such an approach is appropriate for many institutions, but it is insufficient for institutions that, for whatever reasons, are important in specific markets and whose actions affect security prices. For instance, it is well-known that LTCM had extremely large positions in the index option market where it was short. During the crisis, it had little ability to change these positions because it was so large in that market. Further, a large institution can be exposed to predatory trading - i.e., of trades made by others designed to exploit its problems. An example of predatory trading is a situation where traders from other institutions benefit from pushing a price down if they can because it might force a fire sale. Typical risk management models would not account for this. They would not account for the fact that if the institution is large in a market, its losses can lead to more losses. As a firm makes a loss, it may drag down prices for other institutions and make funding more costly across institutions, which can have feedback effects for the institution. Ignoring these potential feedback effects may lead to an understatement of the risk of positions in the event of a crisis. There is little hope for statistical risk models relying on historical data to capture such complicated situations. Rather, a firm has to augment these models with scenario analysis that investigates how crises can unfold and how they will affect it under various assumptions about how it reacts to the crisis. With such scenarios in hand, top management can then understand how crises can endanger the franchise of their institution and how to manage risks before they occur so that they can survive them. Such a scenario approach requires economic and financial analysis. It cannot be done by risk management departments populated by physicists and mathematicians. Such an approach also cannot be successful unless top management believes that the scenarios considered represent legitimate threats to the institution and that the institution has to protect itself against such threats.

drpriyarawal@gmail.com

Chapter-4

Conclusion

Risk management has made considerable progress since 1998. The difficulties of the last year have convinced many observers that somehow there are deep flaws in risk management and that the problems of the last year are partly explained by risk management failures. In this book, we show that one ought to distinguish carefully between risk-taking decisions that unexpectedly lead to losses and risk management assessments of risk. There are many ways that risk management failures can occur, but not every loss reflects a risk management failure. However, risk management practice can be improved by taking into account the lessons from financial crises these crises happen often enough that they have to be carefully modelled and institutions have to focus on scenario analyses that assess the implications of crises for their financial health and survival. Such scenario analyses cannot be built from quantitative models using past data, but instead they must use economic analysis to evaluate the impact of the withdrawal of liquidity and the feedback effects that are common in financial crises. To successfully impact firm strategy, such analyses have to be deeply rooted in a firm's culture and in the strategic thinking of top management. The way forward for India would be to develop an appropriate DRR financing strategy based on a comprehensive risk analysis and needs & gaps assessment. We need to arrive at the appropriate balance of budgetary funding, reserves and contingency funding and risk transfer mechanisms suited to our country. We certainly need to help develop the disaster insurance sector in place of a perpetually underdeveloped disaster insurance market forcing sole reliance on the state exchequer, which is basically a burden on the tax-payer. It must be noted that insurance incentivizes disaster mitigation as premiums are linked to mitigation efforts. In sum, India's achievements so far have been in the areas of techno-legal regime, effective early warning, use of space and ICTs, capacity building, reserve funds and a dedicated response force.

drpriyarawal@gmail.com

www.ingramcontent.com/pod-product-compliance
Lightning Source LLC
Chambersburg PA
CBHW071643170526
45166CB00003B/1410